Cosmos Chronicles
Breakthroughs in Moon Exploration

Elsie Olson

Lerner Publications ◆ Minneapolis

Lerner Publications Company
A division of Lerner Publishing Group, Inc.
241 First Avenue North
Minneapolis, MN 55401 USA

For reading levels and more information, look up this title at www.lernerbooks.com.

Main body text set in Caecilia LT Std 11.25/20
Typeface provided by Adobe Systems.

Photo Acknowledgements
The images in this book are used with permission of: © colorcocktail/iStockphoto, p. 4; © JakeOlimb/iStockphoto, p. 4; © NASA/GSFC/Arizona State University, pp. 4–5, 15 (moon background), 17; © Homann, J. B./Wikimedia Commons, p. 6; © Ann_Mei/iStockphoto, p. 7 (top); © NASA, pp. 7 (bottom left), 8, 9 (1961, 1962, bottom), 10, 13 (bottom), 14, 15 (Apollo 11, 12, 14, 16, and 17 crews), 16, 19 (bottom right, top left), 21 (bottom), 24 (top), 25 (bottom), 26, 27 (top), 28, 29 (bottom); © NASA/JPL, pp. 7 (middle), 27 (Ganymede, Triton); © Wikimedia Commons, pp. 7 (bottom right), 19 (top right); © NASA on The Commons/Flickr, pp. 9 (1969), 20; © NASA/Asif A. Siddiqi, p. 9 (1957); © NASA/Jet Propulsion Laboratory-Caltech, p. 9 (1955); © NASA/Wikimedia Commons, pp. 9 (1966), 13 (top); © NASA Johnson/Flickr, p. 11 (bottom); © NASA/Marshall Space Flight Center/Archive.org, p. 11 (top); © NASA/Neil Armstrong, p. 12; © NASA/JSC, p. 15 (Apollo 15); © Zhang Bo/AP Images, p. 15 (top); © NASA/Goddard Space Flight Center/DLR/ASU, p. 18; © NASA/Apollo 10, p. 19 (bottom left); © NASA/Goddard/Arizona State University, p. 19 (middle left); © NASA/Goddard, p. 21 (top); © NASA/Goddard/University of California, Los Angeles, p. 21 (middle); © Kyodo News/Getty Images, pp. 22–23; © XPRIZE Foundation/Flickr, p. 23; © Steve Jurvetson/Flickr, p. 24 (bottom); © Official SpaceX Photos/Flickr, pp. 25 (top), 29 (top); © NASA, Voyager 2, Copyright Calvin J. Hamilton, p. 27 (Titania); © NASA/JPL-Caltech/SSI, p. 27 (Titan); © NASA/JPL/DLR (German Aerospace Center), p. 27 (Callisto); © NASA/JPL/Space Science Institute, p. 27 (Enceladus).

Cover: © NASA
Design elements: © NASA/JPL-Caltech/STScI/IRAM

Library of Congress Cataloging-in-Publication Data

The Cataloging-in-Publication Data for *Breakthroughs in Moon Exploration* is on file at the Library of Congress.
ISBN 978-1-5415-5596-9 (lib. bdg.)
ISBN 978-1-5415-7369-7 (pbk.)
ISBN 978-1-5415-5644-7 (eb pdf)

Manufactured in the United States of America
1 – CG – 7/15/19

Contents

Meet the Moon!

What exactly is the moon? It's the only natural object that **orbits** Earth. Scientists believe it's been doing so for 4.5 billion years. The moon keeps Earth stable on its axis. This allows for a stable climate. The moon's gravity also causes tides. Without the moon, Earth would be a very different place!

THE MOON AND EARTH

Relationship
If Earth were the size of a nickel, the moon would be the size of a pea.

Distance
The moon is 238,855 miles (384,400 km) from Earth.

Going Around
It takes twenty-seven days for the moon to fully orbit Earth.

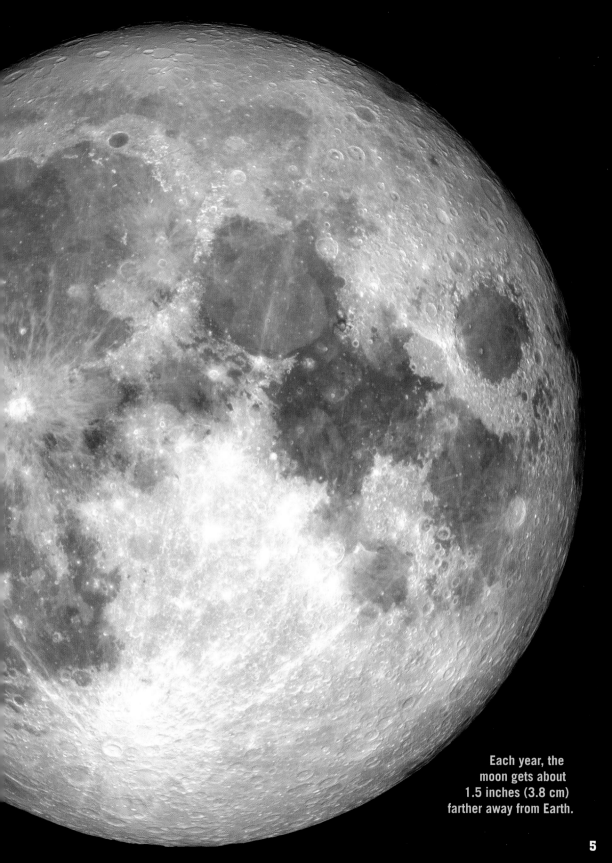

Each year, the
moon gets about
1.5 inches (3.8 cm)
farther away from Earth.

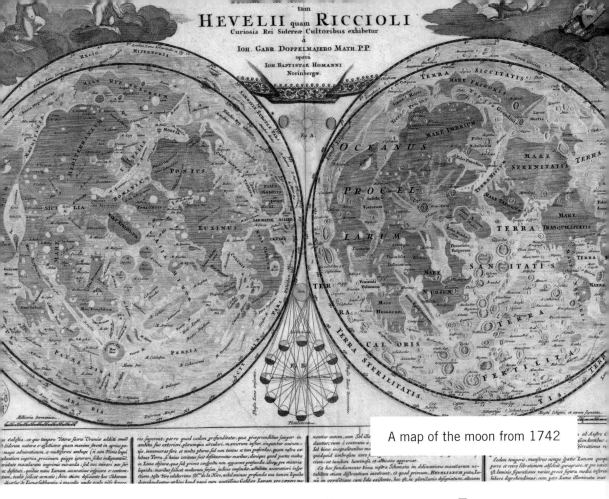

A map of the moon from 1742

Ancient Thoughts and Moon Theories

Humans have come up with many ideas about the moon. Thousands of years ago, they believed the moon was a god or goddess. Some believed the moon had powers over human behavior.

People observed the moon throughout history. But it wasn't until telescopes were invented in the 1600s that astronomers got an up-close look. In the 1950s, the first spacecraft were sent to the moon. Soon after, humans took their first steps on the **lunar** surface.

WHAT ARE HISTORY'S WILDEST MOON THEORIES?

The moon is made of green cheese.

The moon is a hollow spacecraft **inhabited** by aliens.

Full moons can make people go crazy.

WE SEE THE SAME SIDE

The moon rotates at the same rate it orbits Earth. This means the same side of the moon always faces Earth.

The moon as seen from the International Space Station

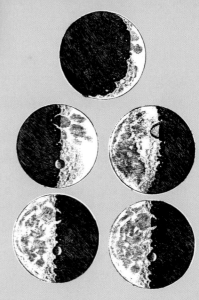

Galileo Galilei's famous 1610 sketches of the moon seen through a telescope

Astronaut Harrison Schmitt stands next to a US flag planted on the moon.

US v. USSR in the Space Race

In the 1950s, the United States and the Soviet Union (USSR) began a conflict known as the Space Race. During this time, each country worked to prove it had the best **technology** by sending **satellites** and spacecraft into space.

1955

US announces plans for the first artificial satellite.

1962

John Glenn becomes the first American to orbit Earth.

1957

Soviets launch the first artificial satellite, Sputnik.

1966

The Soviet Union's Luna 10 is the first spacecraft to orbit the moon.

1961

Soviet Yuri Gagarin becomes the first human to orbit Earth.

1969

US astronauts become the first humans to walk on the moon.

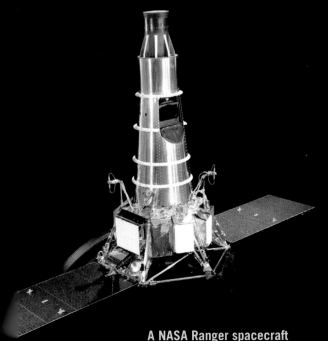

A NASA Ranger spacecraft

MOON CRASHES MEANT TO HAPPEN

NASA launched several Ranger spacecraft to the moon in the 1960s. The **probes** were to take photos of the moon until they crashed into the moon's surface. NASA used the photos to find good landing sites for later missions.

Man Makes History with First Lunar Steps

For most of the Space Race, the Soviets were ahead. But the US pulled ahead on July 20, 1969. That day, astronaut Neil Armstrong became the first human to walk on the moon. Armstrong and fellow astronaut Edwin "Buzz" Aldrin spent several hours walking on the lunar surface.

collecting rock samples on the moon

MORE MANNED MOON LANDINGS

NASA had a total of six successful manned moon landings. A total of twelve Americans have walked on the moon. The final manned mission launched December 7, 1972. No human has visited the moon since.

EXTRATERRESTRIAL OPINION

"That's one small step for a man, one giant leap for mankind."

—US astronaut Neil Armstrong, while taking his first steps on the moon

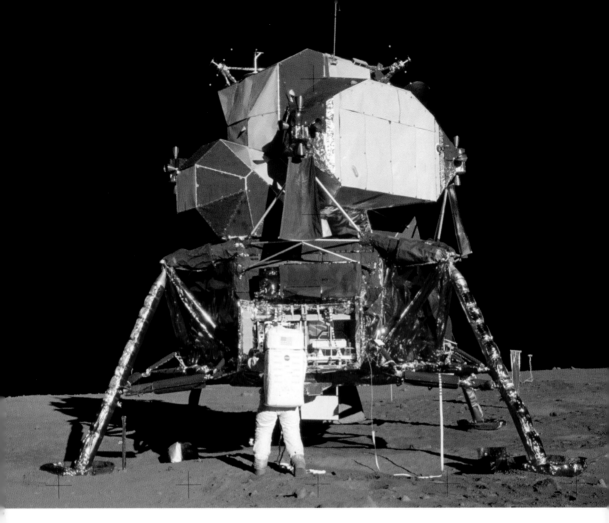

Dusty Moon Walk

When Armstrong took his first steps on the moon in July 1969, he stepped into an environment no human had experienced before. The moon has no oxygen or atmosphere. It has one-sixth of Earth's gravity.

The astronauts walked on a part of the moon called the Sea of Tranquility. This is a plain of volcanic rock covered in fine, powdery dust.

Armstrong and his crewmate Aldrin left deep footprints as they collected moon rock samples and took photos. The astronauts also planted an American flag on the moon.

THOUSANDS OF POUNDS OF HUMAN LITTER ON THE MOON

The astronauts who have set foot on the moon have left behind more than footprints. In fact, scientists think humans have left around 400,000 pounds (181,440 kg) of stuff on the moon! This includes several US flags, ninety-six bags of human waste, an **urn** of human ashes, and more.

Apollo 11 plaque on the moon

EXTRATERRESTRIAL OPINION

"Here men from the planet Earth
first set foot upon the moon
July 1969, A.D.
We came in peace for all mankind"

—plaque left on the moon by Apollo 11 astronauts

Astronaut Alan Shepard encountered boulders and other obstacles during his search for an impact crater on the moon.

Apollo 14 Astronauts Just Miss Incredible View

Astronauts have explored some areas of the moon on foot. In 1971, astronauts Alan Shepard and Edgar Mitchell attempted a lunar hike to a nearby **impact** crater. The crater was about one mile (1.6 km) from where their spacecraft landed.

However, the **terrain** was very hilly, and the astronauts lost sight of the crater during the hike. They turned back rather than risk running out of oxygen. Later images confirmed Shepard and Mitchell were less than three school bus lengths from the crater but couldn't see it!

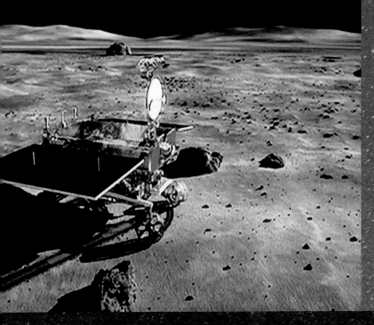

ROBOT TAKES YEARS TO EXPLORE SMALL MOONSCAPE

In 2013, China landed a robotic rover named Yutu on the moon. Yutu was supposed to last only three months. But it continued working for two-and-a-half years! During this time, it traveled just 374 feet (114 m), taking photos and gathering information.

WHERE DID WE WALK?

NASA Moon Landing Dates

APOLLO 15
July 30, 1971
Crew: David R. Scott,
Alfred M. Worden, James B. Irwin

APOLLO 17
December 11, 1972
Crew: Harrison Schmitt,
Eugene A. Cernan,
Ronald E. Evans

APOLLO 12
November 24, 1969
Crew: Alan L. Bean,
Richard F. Gordon,
Charles Conrad, Jr.

APOLLO 14
February 5, 1971
Crew: Alan B. Shepard, Jr.,
Stuart A. Roosa,
Edgar D. Mitchell

APOLLO 11
July 20, 1969
Crew: Neil Armstrong,
Edwin "Buzz" Aldrin, Michael Collins

APOLLO 16
April 21, 1972
Crew: Thomas K. Mattingly II,
John W. Young, Charles M. Duke, Jr.

Modern Missions: Giant Moon Crash Finds Water

NASA scientists long believed some moon craters held ice. In 2009, scientists launched a spacecraft to look for this ice. Once it reached lunar orbit, the spacecraft split in two. As planned, one piece crashed into the moon. This created a cloud of **debris** ten miles (16 km) high.

The second spacecraft piece flew through the cloud. It took measurements and photos before crashing into the moon itself. The data and photos were sent to Earth immediately before the crash.

The data and photos confirmed ice pieces in the cloud. That meant there was frozen water on the moon! One day, this water could be used for drinking or converted into rocket fuel.

Apollo 11 Site

West Crater

200 meters

CITIZEN SCIENTISTS STUDY PHOTOS

From 2010 to 2016, NASA asked citizens to help it study millions of lunar photos. NASA uploaded the photos to a website called Moon Zoo. Website visitors counted craters and boulders in the photos and reported the info to NASA.

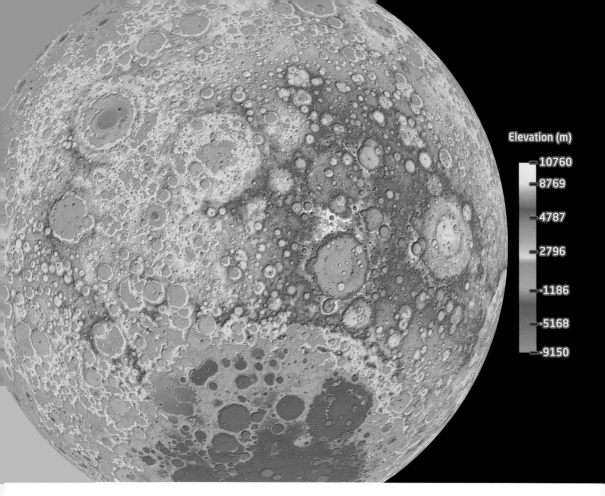

Elevation (m)

10760
8769
4787
2796
-1186
-5168
-9150

Robot Camera Maps the Moon

The moon is our nearest cosmic neighbor. But for many years, scientists had a limited understanding of its surface. That changed in 2009 with NASA's launch of its Lunar Reconnaissance Orbiter (LRO).

A camera on the LRO snapped **high-resolution** photos of the entire lunar surface every month. Meanwhile, a laser measured different features. In 2011, scientists used the data to create the first high-resolution **topographical** moon map!

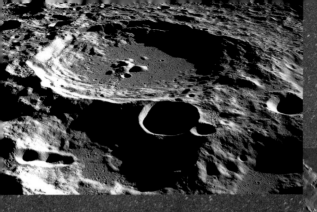

Craters *(left)*: The moon has thousands of craters caused by **meteoroids** hitting it.

Maria *(right)*: Maria are low-lying moon areas and basins that appear dark.

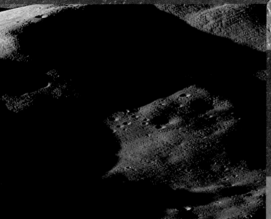

Mountains *(left)*: The moon has many mountains. Its highest point is 35,387 feet (10,786 m). That's higher than Earth's highest point, Mount Everest!

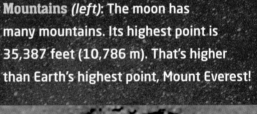

Lava tubes *(right)*: The moon is full of lava tubes. Ancient lava once flowed through these underground tunnels.

Rilles *(left)*: Rilles are long, narrow channels in the lunar surface. Scientists believe some were caused by ancient lava flows.

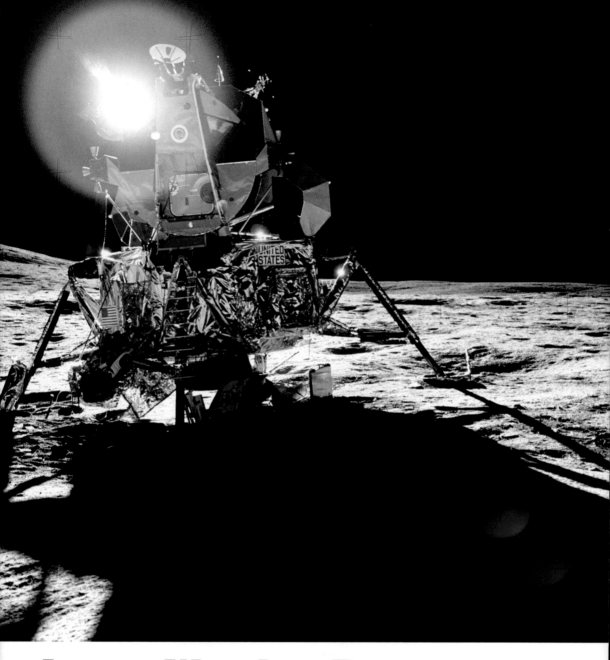

Lunar Weather Report

NASA's 2011 report from its Lunar Reconnaissance Orbiter (LRO) moon mission revealed surprising information about the lunar weather. This included areas of eternal sunshine, super-cold craters, and extreme temperatures.

A SUNNY SOUTH POLE

The moon's south pole receives continuous sunshine for 243 days a year! The region is never in darkness for more than twenty-four hours at a time.

LRO GETS CHILLY

NASA found the coldest place in the solar system at the bottom of the moon's Hermite Crater. The temperature there was -415 degrees Fahrenheit (-248 °C)!

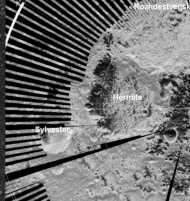

NO ATMOSPHERE

The moon has no atmosphere. It cannot hold heat or cool down. During the day, it reaches 253 degrees Fahrenheit (123 °C). At night, temperatures drop to -387 degrees Fahrenheit (-233 °C).

Spacesuits were designed to protect astronauts from extreme temperatures during moonwalks.

MOON CHALLENGE

Will There Be a New Space Race?

In 2007, tech company Google challenged private companies to land a spacecraft on the moon. Known as the Lunar XPRIZE, teams could compete to win $30 million! To win, the spacecraft had to travel 1,640 feet (500 m) on the lunar surface and send a live broadcast back to Earth.

The deadline was March 31, 2018. By 2017, there were five competing teams. In the end, all teams missed the deadline. No team claimed the prize. But several teams continued to move forward with their projects.

was a finalist in the Google Lunar XPRIZE competition.

EXTRATERRESTRIAL OPINION
"The day before something is truly a breakthrough, it's a crazy idea."
——Peter Diamandis, chairman of the

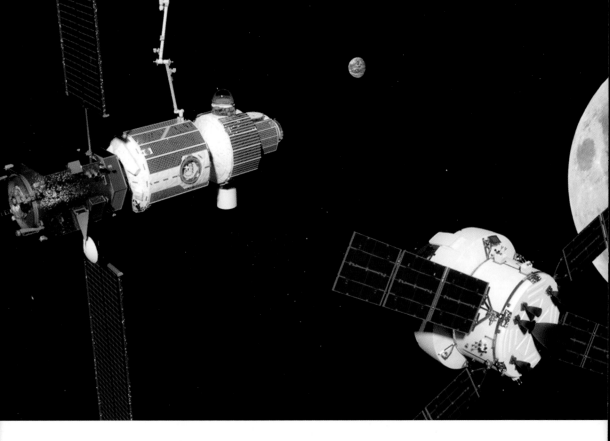

Lunar Outposts Planned

In 2018, NASA scientists announced plans to build a Lunar Orbital Platform-Gateway along with several other countries. This space station would orbit the moon. Astronauts would live and work on the station. The station would make missions to the lunar surface much easier. It would also pave the way for future missions to Mars and beyond!

EXTRATERRESTRIAL OPINION
"Becoming a space-faring civilization is one of those things that makes you excited about the future."
—Elon Musk, founder of US aerospace company SpaceX

SPACEX SHOOTS FOR THE MOON

US aerospace company SpaceX is developing Big Falcon Rocket (BFR). BFR is being made to carry passengers to the moon and back to Earth. It will be the first reusable rocket. Other rockets can only be used once. Reusing rockets would lower the cost of space travel.

One day, NASA may build an outpost on the lunar surface.

Mars has two small, irregularly shaped moons called Phobos and Deimos.

Room for Many Moons

Earth isn't the only planet with a moon. In fact, our solar system has hundreds of moons. Jupiter alone has seventy-nine! Astronomers have even found tiny moons orbiting some asteroids. Moons are many sizes and have varied terrain. Some are rocky, others are icy. Scientists believe some of Jupiter's moons may even contain oceans beneath their ice-covered surfaces.

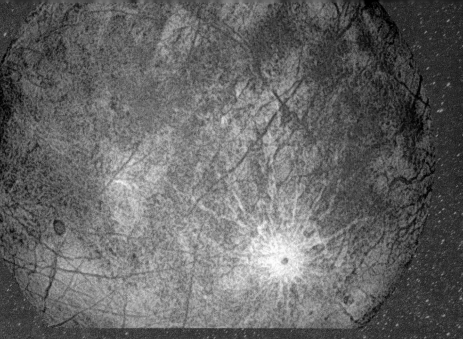

Scientists believe there may be an ocean on Jupiter's moon, Europa, beneath a thick layer of ice. They think this ocean could possibly support life.

IS THERE LIFE ON OTHER MOONS?

Astrobiologists think some of Jupiter's and Saturn's moons might be the best places to look for alien life. Many of these moons have water or ice. Water is **essential** for life on Earth and scientists think it may be for alien life too.

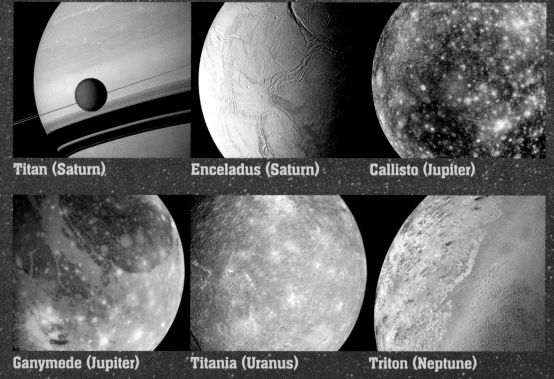

Titan (Saturn)   Enceladus (Saturn)   Callisto (Jupiter)

Ganymede (Jupiter)   Titania (Uranus)   Triton (Neptune)

Cosmos Exclusive!

What's new and upcoming in moon exploration?

A lunar outpost would be the first step to permanently changing the moon's climate.

Can the Moon Be the Next Florida?

Some scientists believe humans could alter the moon to be suitable for life. Humans could tow icy **comets** and crash them into the moon. The impacts would tilt the moon on its axis, creating seasons. Then humans would plant trees and other plants. Certain scientists say the moon's climate would end up being like Florida's! However, this process would take hundreds of years, and humans do not have the needed technology yet.

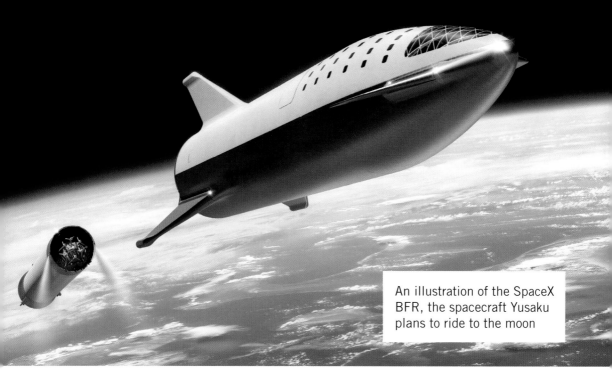

An illustration of the SpaceX BFR, the spacecraft Yusaku plans to ride to the moon

Billionaire to Buy Moon Vacation

SpaceX founder Elon Musk believes the future of space travel is **tourism**. In 2018, Musk announced company plans to make Japanese billionaire Yusaku Maezawa the first space tourist. A one-week mission is planned for 2023. SpaceX spacecraft will carry Yusaku and guests he chooses around the moon before returning to Earth.

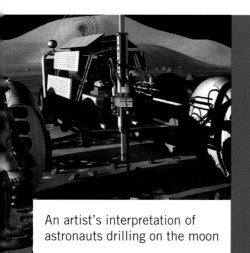

An artist's interpretation of astronauts drilling on the moon

Mining on the Moon

The moon is full of elements that are valuable to humans. Helium-3 could be especially valuable. It can be used as a clean-burning fuel that could help power technology. US Aerospace company Moon Express is working to develop a plan to mine the moon.

Glossary

astrobiologists: scientists who study life in the universe

comets: bright celestial bodies with long tails of light

debris: pieces of something that has been broken or destroyed

essential: necessary or very important

high-resolution: showing a great amount of detail

impact: the forceful striking of one thing against another

inhabited: lived in

lunar: of or having to do with the moon

meteoroids: a small, rocky, or metallic body moving in the solar system

orbits: travels in a circular path around something, especially a planet or the sun

probes: tools or devices used to explore or examine something

satellites: spacecraft that are sent into orbit around Earth or another body

technology: the use of science and engineering to do technical things

terrain: an area of land

topographical: detailed and descriptive of the physical features of an area, including rivers, lakes, hills, mountains, and more

tourism: the practice of traveling for entertainment or recreation. A person who does this traveling is a tourist.

urn: a type of vase that is often used to contain ashes of the dead after cremation

BOOKS

Bredeson, Carmen. *Exploring the Moon.* New York: Enslow, 2016.
Learn about lunar phases and exploration and careers that involve studying the moon.

Mahoney, Emily Jankowski. *What Is on the Far Side of the Moon?* New York: Gareth Stevens Publishing, 2018.
Find interesting facts about the far side of the moon, moon craters and moon seas, and more.

Nagelhout, Ryan. *What Is a Moon?* New York: Britannica/Rosen, 2015.
Read scientists' ideas about how the moon was formed and learn about other planets' moons.

WEBSITES

Ducksters—The Phases of the Moon for Kids
https://www.ducksters.com/science/phases_of_the_moon.php
Read about the moon's phases and the lunar calendar.

Kids Astronomy—The Moon
https://kidsastronomy.com/solar-system/the-moon
Explore tons of information about the moon, including its size, terrain, and how it affects Earth's tides.

National Geographic Kids—Facts About the Moon!
https://www.natgeokids.com/au/discover/science/space/facts-about-the-moon/
Discover ten supercool facts about the moon.